Heart Haiku

Alaska Inspired Photos and Poems
By
Dwayne Cole

Front Cover

Gulls nesting as one
Nature's love is rock solid
Heart to heart

Kachemak Bay, Alaska, near Halibut Cove.
Haiku inspired by sea stack with heart shaped opening.
Nature is awesome! To cruise in Kachemak Bay, is a shimmering,
luminous experience with bright beauty.
All photos are mine unless otherwise indicated.

Dedication

This book is dedicated to Beth, my wife,
whose editorial skills are invaluable.
I am also grateful for our Alaska family,
Ken, Kim, Cole, and Paxton. Without their invitation
to share in their Alaska adventure; and their daily love
for the last decade, this book, *Heart Haiku*,
would not have been possible. In the three simple lines
of the small haiku, a sensation of largeness is created.
Beth and my loving family are always in that heart space
inspiring me, along with the healing presence of beautiful
Alaska nature scenes. I am also grateful for the daily wonder
I experienced in our grandchildren, Cole and Paxton.
Their artwork and poems helped me rediscover
a child's wonder in my daily life. The cloud photo says—

Heart Haiku wonder
Family hearts merging as one
Miracle of love

Introduction

Sun ray needles
Stitching together new day
Light for our pathway

Heaven's lure
Glorifies the present
Bringing much joy

Come shine on our world
Illumine with heaven's light
Showing us the way

Beth and I enjoy poetry and wanted to share verses
with our grandchildren, as a way to nurture openness
with the beauty and wonder of nature. The three simple lines

of the small haiku, have traditionally been seen
as a good place to start teaching children a love of poetry.
Haiku uses inspiring nature scenes that enrich the lives
of teacher and student. Our grandchildren's artwork
and poems helped us re-discover a child's wonder
in our lives. Seeing the sparkle in their eyes helped us
to see with the eyes of a child. The tears of joy washed
away some of life's travel stains that cloud our vision.
The wonder of a child blossomed anew in us,
becoming fertile ground for tender teachings.

I grew up in a farmhouse that was built from timber grown on
the farm. When we used a tree, we planted or cultivated
another, linking me to the magic of trees. My childhood
bedroom shared with 6 brothers was a porch closed in for
sleeping, and at times you could count stars through the roof
and exposed rafters. My 6 sisters had a nice bedroom they   shared.
Mindful of that farmhouse, I wrote this haiku—

> always very welcome
> snowflakes falling on bed quilts
> little boys' delight

Haiku began in thirteenth-century Japan as the opening phrase
of renga, a long poem. The short haiku broke away from renga
in the sixteenth century. Haiku, using provocative, colorful
images, focuses on a brief moment in time when we slow down
and see nature scenes like an alpenglow sunrise or sunset
transforming the whole sky. Haiku has a deep appreciation
of nature. Alaskans are closely related to luminous sparkling
mountains, streams, and wildlife. Thus, haiku is especially
suited to speak of the heartbeat of Alaska.

Haiku often ends with a surprising sense of enlightenment.
It is in this aha moment, in empathy, that the songbird sings
our heart awake, revealing truths from unknown realms.
We see with new eyes and hear with new ears, moving into
new adventures. We may not know where we are going, but
we feel a new way has been opened. Kindness is in that Way.

The format of haiku is three lines, with the first and third lines each having 5 syllables, and the second line having 7 syllables. However, the emphasis is on three lines with an economy of words, not a total of 17 syllables. The syllable count may vary in each line—brevity that avoids overuse of metaphors and simile is key. Sensory experience is the goal.

I use Alaska nature photographs I have taken as inspiration for my haiku. Poetry inspired by art has been described as ekphrastic—meaning, to draw descriptive images out of the art. The haiku and the photograph share the same space and often compliment each other. but not to explain one another. In some instances, the haiku and the photograph have little to do with one another. Each can stand alone. Otherwise it would mean that one has been added because the other is not complete or adequate to stand alone.

At the heart of nature haiku is a deep feeling of beauty. The wish to live and experience this beauty and wonder is visible in all living entities. In sharing this beauty, we experience enlivenment—The deep meaning of life. Nature throbs with the desire to live. Haiku captures this beauty and sense of adventurous enlightenment, luring us toward more meaningful lives.

One should pause after reading each haiku. Then you might want to read the haiku again, seeing new meaning. When moving to the next one, there may be no connection from one to the other. Yet, sometimes they may follow in logical sequence.

Dazzling Alpenglow
Playing music of angels
Pulls on our heart strings

Artist's palette
Red silver pink salmon
All day and night glow

King salmon leaping
In gray glacier melt streams
Brown bears growing fat

Storing

Hibernation

Energy

Tossing and turning—
Moonless midnight dreams.
Look, Heaven's light!

Santa's prize—
Ribbons of northern light.
Grandchildren dancing!

Northern lights calling
Lover standing at the door
Singing a love song

My heart is yearning
for your magical colors.
Shine shine shine on me!

Beauty unfolds
Rows of golden mountains
Alaska's treasures

Setting sun magic
Turning mountains into gold
Shine, shine on us

Two hundred and fifty miles
Alaskan golden wonders
Chugach mountain range

With mountains glowing
Little nuthatch catches fire
My soul draws flame

I wake to magic
World captivating beauty
Arrayed in wonder

On artist's palette
The blending of earthly light
And spiritual glory

seeking to find self
in daily entanglements
reality check

silver birch trees
shadowed into children's toys
by looming mountains

Grasping shadows,
the poet finds substance.
Essence of universe!

Drawn into mystery,
I find my place in cosmos.
Glorious dreams!

So beautifully,
chickadee floats to seed dish.
Heaven's messenger!

Flying in to bring
love energies from on high—
A twinkle in eye!

Wise Bird Ways

These hardy little birds stay in Alaska
all year, surviving -40 degrees nights by
fluffing feathers into down sleeping bag
and sleeping in tree cavities or snow tunnels.
On coldest nights, they shiver to create body warmth.
They must find food soon on waking to restore energy
and create body heat or freeze. They store food in secret
places all summer and fall for these cold nights.
It warms my heart to give them sunflower heart seeds.

Heart birds come awake
It is -18 on snowy deck
Love gifts warm

pure poetry

flower petals falling

feel the breeze

Grosbeak Sermon
Sharing sunflower heart seeds
God cares for birds

God cares
for you
and me

wings of inspiration

eyes spinning universe

hearts beating as one

The teleology of the universe moves toward Beauty.
—Based on A. N. Whitehead

Two Grosbeak Tankas

Welcome pine grosbeaks,
gracing our chaotic world.
Wings of inspiration.
Love songs from unknown realms
moving the world toward Beauty.

Grosbeak wings whisper—
Messages from unknown realms.
Secrets bind as one.
Nature's wonders give us life,
Life for all of God's children.

(Tanka is poem that starts as a haiku
and contains two additional lines of
seven syllables each, but can vary
in number of syllables.)

Rose blossoms falling,
spinning and whiffling around—
Look, redpolls are back!

Raspberry blossoms
falling from bramble bushes—
Whiffle, fly back up.

Who gives you secrets?
Cares for your daily needs?
Heaven's tenderness!

Alaskan redpoll,
a small brown and gray songbird,
male tips a red cap.

Redpolls like new buds
fill bare branches with color.
Spring's bright heralds!

Temps below zero,
hardy little redpoll says—
It will be alright!

Nature prepares
a throat pouch lunch box
for storing life seeds.

In the long cold nights
redpolls fluff contour feathers.
A snug sleeping bag!

Redpolls whiffle down
adding heavenly sunlight.
Leaves on bare branches.

Look at the songbirds.
God lovingly cares for them.
God takes care of us.

—Based on Matthew 6:25-26

Nature drops love notes
on wings of inspiration.
God's beauty enfold.

By every doorway
Tub for knee high hiking boots
Winter snow falling

The year is fleeing
Beard is white and falling down
Wrapping presents now

Steller's jay prancing
Ministerial robe flapping
My associate

Preaching on deck rail
Steller's jay exultation
Welcomes the new day

I took these trumpeter swan photos as Beth and I walked
at Potter Marsh in Anchorage, AK. Wrote the haiku to Beth,
my love, since our first meeting in a seminary Greek class
in 1964 and marriage in 1965.

float on cool water
like graceful trumpeter swans
bob along with me

Dip in the cool pond
Nestled in musical reeds
Sleep the night away

Float by you forever
My graceful trumpeter swan
Nestled in our love

As I saw the arctic tern soaring, I asked, how do these champion migrators manage to travel 47,000 miles each year from the Arctic to the Antarctic. Tossed about with icy gales and shaken by storm currents. They just appear as if conjured by Mother Nature's magic wand. Master mariners following invisible compass.

Birds are ideas
Music of the soul
Arctic tern soaring

Language of nature
An elixir of wonder
Migration champion

The tern teaches us
How to live free of burdens
Incarnating purity

The Moose photos and haiku are taken from my book,
BEARS AND MOOSE OF ALASKA: Nature Poetry.

Rutting rack ready
Brown grass waving love notes
Sniff the air

Moose with full rack
Legend among the wolf pack
Ready for rut game

Rutting game over,
I won the victory prize.
Just adore my gifts!

Twin moose calves bounce
as toy boats on the green sea.
Remember to breathe!

Young male moose
munching water lilies.
Blue water rippling.

Mother and daughter
downloading genetic code.
I am yours, you're mine.

Seeing the love dance,
my lips whispered joyful songs.
All's right with the world.

Green fields are dancing.
All nature feels the rhythm.
My heart skips a beat!

Feel love tango
Waltz of the universe
Feel family love

Feeling this connection was to sense the joy of being alive.
Contributing to nature's beauty is the hope of accepting all
persons as precious and bring healing to our broken world.

Bedded in the snow
White blanket covers all
Dreams taking shape

Wrapped in snow blanket
Mother to be moose dreaming
Need dandelions to munch

Newborn moose calf
rising out of green sea.
Decked in dandelions.

Stands on first day
Thirty-five pound prize
Mother watches bear

Mother on alert.
Calf nibbles dandelions.
Mothers are awesome!

Snowshoe hare eating
catkins from cottonwood trees.
A purple delight.

I bring a flower
The prettiest I could find
Give kindness to all

God has spoken:
Be kind to my children!

Based on Isaiah 40:1-2   D. Cole

God has spoken.
Be kind to my little ones—
Heaven is waiting!

(Taken from my book, *Kindness Is Every Step: Photos and Poems.*)

Autumn leaves fall
on fast moving stream.
They fly up again!

On a cold winter day
Mountain and sky caress
All creation glows

Golden clouds catch fire
Red-breasted nuthatch draws flame
My soul is warmed

Red-breasted Nuthatch

Angels at play
Flower blossoms falling
They fly up again

Heart to Heart Haiku

Fingertip felt heart
Beating twice as fast as mine
I took wings and flew

Trust is bird eating
Sunflower heart seeds from hand
Remember to breathe

(Taken from my book, *WINGS OF INSPIRATION: Photos and Poems.*)

Mark Houston
My salmon fishing buddy
Friends are forever

Blue skies smile
on glacier melt Copper river
Home of king salmon

My friend, Mark, invited me
to go dip netting for salmon
in the Copper River, Chitina, Ak.
Each resident in Alaska is allowed
to dip net 25-30 wild salmon each year
to fill their freezers for family use.
When we eat salmon that have navigated
oceans and rivers, leaped waterfalls,
and escaped the jaws of brown bears—
The salmon, the oceans, and rivers
are all within us and become part of us.

With our cooler in line to catch first boat
taking us to a choice dip netting spot
at break of day, we went to sleep in the car,
reclined in the front seats. We were awakened
by a bear pounding on the front grill and
hood. The car was rocking so much that my first
thought was that we were having an earthquake.
Then I saw the bear!

He was eating insects off the grill guard. We blew
the horn and he walked by my window, stared at me
eyeball to eyeball, not more than one foot away;
and fortunately, he went over to another car and
did the same trick. He could have easily broken
the car window and had a larger meal.

When the sun came up, we each dip netted our
25 salmon, filleted them, and went home to fill
our freezers. Alaska is wild! It has one bear
for every 5 persons and one moose for every
4 persons.

Thankfully, bears prefer salmon and moose
more than people.

Our body is nourished.
Our soul is enraptured by mystery.
Blue skies are smiling.

From his rock perch
Bear cub watches mama fishing
Salmon for lunch

Some sing to entertain
I sing to keep bears away
I sing from treetops

Brown bear cubs tumble
Announcing spring miracles
My spirit is revived

Bears walk in our yard
like they own it, and they do.
Welcome mat is out.

Polar Bear in Alaska Zoo, Haibun

Polar bears in Arctic regions of Alaska are in a
period of decline— Estimated to be 40 percent
between 2001-2010, dropping from 1,500 to 900 bears.
Because of loss of their sea ice habitat
resulting from climate change, polar bears
were listed as a threatened species in the US
under the Endangered Species Act in May 2008.

Although they are flexible, adaptable, and smart,
the long-term outlook in the face of sea ice loss
does not bode well for the bears.
Current projections predict that by 2050,
sea ice in the Arctic will be gone,
and in another several decades polar bears
in Alaska may follow.

>Bored and growing old
>Climate change is real for me
>Would like to live free

spring flowers so sweet
all of nature is smiling
bees coming to greet

Kindergarten nursery
Filled with smiling faces
Nature's beauties

Go into garden
Hear nature singing
Find your song again

Magpie is Haiku

waddling penguin
in magpie spying disguise
read my grey lips

nest building time
blue-green tail feathers quivering
love adventures wait

evolution art
nature's array of colors
priceless treasure trove

bees sipping nectar
or jinni spinning spinning
in elfin garden

wonderful to be
emerging from the beehive
fall in honey cup

just sighing humming
sipping from the flower cup
making honeycomb

how do little bees
know what part to play
storing pollen grains

following nectar trails
filling baskets on hind legs
flying to hive drunk

Being beckoned.
Climb the spruce tree and touch me.
I'm the iCloud person.

standing in half light
waiting for the full moonlight
love is in my sight

The tundra sparkles
with colorful wildflowers
Summer surprises

Glacial melt water
falls and swells swift flowing streams
flow swiftly to-sea   D. Cole

Sunrise will not write
fears of a moonless midnight
Warmth of new day

{Photo taken from my book, *Alpenglow Miracles: Fire Dance of Wonder.)*

With wingtips afire

Eagle soars in Alpenglow

My soul catches flame

moose came up to door
ate pumpkin without asking
scarecrow grinning

Oh, please moose
Don't eat me for a treat
Straw is dry

Blue flower unfolds,
beautiful butterfly.
Fluttering my heart!

Flowers shine starlight
Announcing spring miracles
Find wonder again

Should I go in or
not go into this neat school?
Kids say, all welcome!

We will make for you
a twiggy stand alone desk.
What a fun school day!

(Moose photo taken at grandchildren's school, and first published with
poem in my book, *BEARS AND MOOSE OF ALASKA: Nature Poetry.*)

Alaska's 7.2 earthquake—
Panic crawls under table.
The stars are shining!

7.2 earthquake
Spruce limbs quivering
Reach out to me

Mother and daughter
downloading survival codes.
I'm yours, you are mine.

White paper birch bark.
Sketch pad for glowing red leaves.
Quiet, Nature's art show!

Happy is honeybee
Collecting nectar so free
Caring for hive

Fireweed is glowing
Soon be all the way to top
Snow is coming soon

Snowshoe hare dancing
in sunshine with stocking feet
my winter day treat.

Flowers whisper love
Sun and moon glows in each one
Stars of wonder

flowers thrive kissing
Soft rays of the morning sun
Sipping morning tea

Moose with a full rack
A legend among wolf pack
Rose eying his date

Ripe to mate
He always said
I'll be right back

standing in half-light
waiting for the full moonlight
love is in my sight

moose contemplating
rut time is drawing near
brown grass waving

(Moose photo and poems from my book,
*BEARS AND MOOSE OF ALASKA:
Nature Poetry*).

Two Chugach mountain peaks in Alaska, with a touch of alpenglow, calling to memory Artemis, Greek goddess of mountains. The Chugach range is 250 miles long and 60 miles wide. These mountains get an average of 66.6 feet of snow each year, more than anywhere else in the world. The range runs behind our condo with marvelous views. They inspired the haiku below, as they do much of my writing. They also bring wild Alaska with its towering trees, moose, and bears into view from our yard, as can be seen in my books, *BEARS AND MOOSE OF ALASKA: Nature Poetry, Alpenglow Miracles: Fire Dance of Wonder,* and *Clouds of Inspiration.*

Goddess Artemis
Lies basking in evening sun
Clouds coyly blush

Chickadees have been seen as a symbol of good fortune.
I wrote the haiku below as my wish for all lovers of nature—

Coming to say Hi
Bringing you good luck wishes
With loving eyes

Sitting on my deck
Listening to chickadees chirp
Song of universe

Iditarod Sled Dog Race

The winning racer of the Alaska Iditarod Sled Dog Race from Willow to Nome takes about 10 days, plus or minus a few hours, traveling approximately 1,000 miles. Sometimes the temperature is as low as -40. Cold temperatures bother the mushers more than the dogs.

There are strict rules in caring for the dogs, with required rest times at check points. They must take one 24 hours rest time and two 8 hours rest times. All dogs are examined at rest points by volunteer veterinarians.

Racers range in age from early twenties to eighty. The winner gets a new pickup truck and as much as $50,000 cash prize. The last racer to finish wins the Red Lantern Award, sometimes as much as 10 days after the winner. I had to write at least 3 haiku in honor of the big race.

nice day in the snow
wish you were all here in place
to see the dog race

up the hill such fun
the run has just now begun
scary going down

look at those tongues
wagging down the sled dog trail
dogs are hot and ready

(I took the photos at the 2017 ceremonial start of Iditarod in Anchorage.)

When elephants fly
they can crash into
spruce trees.

D. Cole

(Humor is one way of cultivating awareness in nature. These snow elephant haiku seek to open hearts to the wonder of humor.)

when elephants fly
Dumbo lands in tall spruce tree
Horns blow merry tune

The next two lynx photos are among my favorites taken on our family's mini-farm in Anchorage, Alaska. I wrote the haiku to nurture beauty and wonder with our grandchildren. Beauty and wonder are a language children understand. Carry your child wonder with you and you will never grow old.

Beautiful lynx
Descendant of the Sphinx
Golden eyes a prize

Tree full of surprise
Glad the day is not yet night
Glowing eyes cause fright

A beautiful lynx
Descendant of the Sphinx
Magic pulled out of a hat

It looked as though
Trees were shedding redpoll leaves
Swirl and dance my soul

Look, trees shedding leaves
They swirl around and around
They fly up again

Cotton Candy Sunset
Snowy blue shades are drawn
Blushing pink the night

Hungry snowshoe hare
Saw Snowman's long carrot nose
Yummy in tummy

Photo of bleeding heart bush and poems are taken from my book,
Poet of the Universe, pages 92-93. My vision of beauty and
goodness expressed as kindness in all my books and poems
are especially intended to include all who suffer. I tenderly care
for my bleeding heart plant, growing by my condo, as a beautiful
reminder to show compassion for the suffering of others.

Hurting hearts abound
Jesus' heart pierced by a sword
Bleeding for everyone

On our farm chickens run wild. Loving brown mother hen looks on brood of multi-colored chicks with caring eyes and protective angel wings. Like caregivers everywhere.

Color of her brood
Sends message to broken world
Love knows no color

As the sun set,
I heard the mountains whispering—
Art show in progress!

Big Rock Candy Mountain
Blesses bedroom window tonight
Our special delight

Sandra Felix
Photo

Zest for beauty is experienced as one tastes with the wise little elf
water drops on flower petals. The essence of the universe
is in that sweetness.

Pink flower unfolds
like beautiful butterfly
Fluttering my heart

Wildflowers opening
A Kingdom not of this world
Bees sipping nectar

I watched in horror as eagle swoops down on a raft of ducklings, taking one in its sharp talons. I wrote this haibun to process my anguish. I never said nature is always kind.

Symbol of empires
Kings Prophets Evangelists
Uprooting, planting

Prepared for lift off
Duckling in claws breathing last
Eaglets to feed

Growing fast
Mystery of nature unfolds
Nature not always kind

But oh the beauty
Young eaglets spreading wings
Wish to be eagle

Cool raindrops
Filling flower cup
Soul tranquilizer

Wildflower garden
Playground of Tolkien's elves
Love blossoms

Waterfall from clouds
Clouds from waterfalls
United as one

Dwayne Cole

I stand in awe
One with the magical force
Pulse of universe

Kittiwake

A small gull of Alaska,
named for its nasal
"ki-ti-waak" call notes.

Seldom comes to land,
but knows how to pick
a home so grand.

Nesting crevices
of the rocky sea stack cliffs
carved by waterfalls.

Pure glacial water
baptizes the baby gulls
The heart of nature

Pierced by rays from heaven
You cannot hear the raucous
Joyful tune without feeling

Wonder of rebirth
Feeling of precious newness
Pristine aliveness

Sparkling waterfalls
speak poetic ecology
Pristine aliveness

This is life
Celestial ecstasy
Delight of eternity

Tumbling waterfalls
Forward moving universe
Gulls cry with joy

(Photos taken at Whittier, Alaska.)

Lavender flowers
I erase and write again
A garden blooms

Gentle care of God
Butterflies sipping nectar
God's glory is here

Jumble of fireweed
Reaching for the stars
Bees making honey

A field of fireweed
Smile of a grandchild
Spring's tender gifts

(Photo of my wife, grandchild, and daughter)

Icing on my cake
The candles that light my days
Smiles of love and joy

Nature Heals

fly fishing at Lake Clark
orthopedic surgeon son-in-law
taking healing break

Some of my choice fishing flies tied while teaching my grandchildren to tie flies. I started with them when they had to sit in my lap to reach the flytying vice.

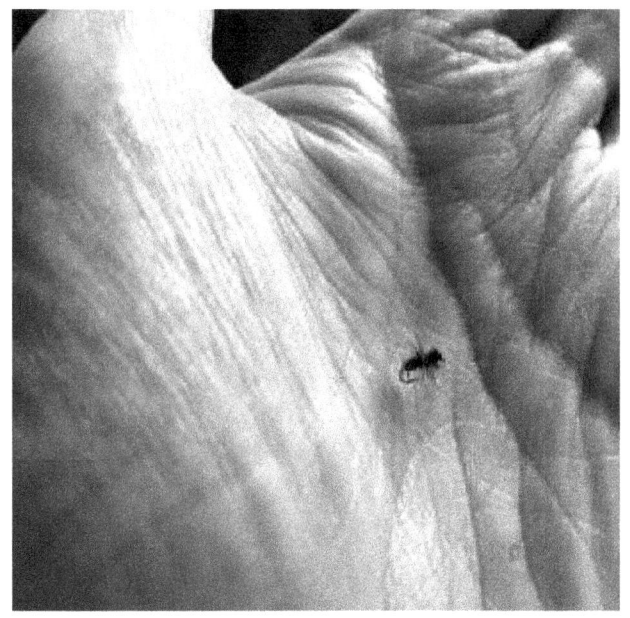

Fishing Fly Zinger

Tied a dozen flies
to restock my flyfish box.
Heart haiku zingers.

Who knows for sure
what the trout thinks
when it softly plops.

If I spot a rainbow
sipping midges with a splash,
will think, a big one!

One day soon I'll see
a rainbow trout swirl and splash—
Hear dinner bell ring!

When I saw the cloud photo I took, it looked like the face of Thor in Norse Mythology. Thor, the hammer god sends thunder and lightning. Storms raging and blowing his large curly beard. In myth, Thor is the strongest of all gods and men. Don't make Thor angry.

> myths that never were
> yet illumine what is
> and always will be

Moose came to window.
Stared at us eyeball to eyeball.
We were here first!

Moose adds playful mood
to an adventurous day.
Grandchildren happy!

Fireweed blossoms climb
Higher upon the stalk each day
Summer sun sinking

Fireweed blossoms fall
On the green grass bed cover
Star dust in moonlight

Sit among flowers.
Touch tassels of Jesus' robe.
Feel God's love and care.

Sit among flowers.
Touch Mother Teresa's robe.
Care for poor children.

Sit among flowers.
Touch the Buddha's simple robe.
Teach kindness for all.

Each little flower
is part of total beauty
of the universe.

Purity of heart
determined by how we treat
little flowers.

Grosbeak

From all directions
Gifts from heaven are calling
Love is in the air

Nature is the poet.
Birds are poems nature writes—
Spreading songs of joy!

Redpolls are living Blossoms
Borne by nature's bountiful beauty
Tenderness and care

From all directions
Raspberry blossoms falling
Nature spreading love

Stars of heaven fall
On sunflower heart seed dish
Warmth on snowy days

Has spring come yet?
Look at my Alaska yard.
Snow is belly deep!

Snow is belly deep.
Thermometer reads -12.
Frozen twig breakfast.

Rays of sunlight
shine through the leafless limbs.
Can spring be far behind?

Inside every home
Plastic tub for hiking boots
Snow knee deep

Picture speaks poem
Look at my snow covered lips
Words are not needed

Clothed in tassel
Nature's beauty is glowing
Shake your sass

Moose rose-eyeing mate
Setting sun warming his back
Waiting for twilight

Rut season is here
Let the mating begin
Hope it never ends

Sunshine of trusting
Warm hearts are glowing brightly
Remember to breathe

Overwhelm me muse
Wings glowing in heaven's light
Mystery abounding

Coming from journey
A migration on the wind
Magic of springtime

My life will never be the same after this glowing experience.
The little chickadee, bringer of good wishes, sat on my
fingertips, with eyes shining, looked deep into my eyes,
and took my heart seeds. I felt great joy!

snowshoe camouflage
environmental wonder
hide-n-seek winner

A favorite game
the snowshoes and magpies
play often in our yard.

From gray to white crown,
to eyes spinning universe—
Beauty all around!

Dwayne Cole

Boreal Chickadee

Wisdom of bird songs
What will you write for today
Songs that flutter the heart

Wisdom of bird songs
What will you sing for today
Life's a precious gift

D. Cole

The Denali Arctic ground squirrel lives among the rocks in a burrow. This provides protection from the Arctic fox who sees it as a good meal. Some Alaska natives used them as a ruff on their parka cuff. They hibernate during the 8 winter months in Denali.
Maybe 5,750 hours of beauty sleep is why they are so cute.

I stay close to home
I'm a ruff for parka cuff
I love Denali

Arctic Ground Squirrel
Warming in bright sunlight
Denali delight

Beth walked a little too long in the snow
and turned into a snow angel. d. cole

Walk in unison.
The world a single shrine—
Home of the elves!

Walk in unison.
The world a single temple—
Home of snow angels!

19 below zero
Icicles crack and pop
Waking Yeti

Cold snow blowing
Totem pole creaks and moans
Shadows in moonlight

Wildflowers adorning
pathway to summer fragrance.
Bull Moose just ate one!

Little baby grebe,
don't despair and cry out so loud.
Papa is here now!

Look, dragonflies,
landing on a lily pad.
From antiquity.

Beautiful dragonflies!
Four rainbow wings glittering.
The grebe just ate one!

Hold on for the ride.
Sex in the garden is grand.
How much can love stand!

Make joyful poems
Full of mystery and wonder
Dragonfly magic

(Geneticists believe that dragonflies are laggards
and have not changed in the last two hundred million years.
See my book, Dragonfly Magic.)

Spring is really here!
The Mew Gulls have returned
Giving mating calls

Amazing star journey
Travel many miles each year
Spruce trees waiting

Radar accuracy
Return to where they hatched
No place like home

Coming today tonight
Mew gulls filling Baxter Bog
All are courting

In my condo yard,
beautiful pushki blossoms.
The moose just ate one!

Sitting side by side,
mother daughter contemplate.
I'm yours, you are mine!

no school today
poop on pencil work
many games to play

In the melting snow,
snowshoes dancing joyfully.
Oh, happy playmates!

Dwayne Cole

Two snowshoe hares were chasing each other all around the yard. The female moved so fast she was a blur. To preserve their privacy, I am not posting the wild sexy photos. This photo says it is love haiku.

As darkness moves in
Annual love affair begins
Dancing with great joy

Kicking their heels high
Spring love works magic in snow
Nature is so grand

Photos

are

haiku

Molting is complete
Snowshoe nibbling dandelion
Lynx patiently waits

On the mountain tops,
the sun suddenly shines bright.
Look, heaven's pathway!

Come shine on me.
Illumine me with heaven's light.
Hallelujah!

Soaring in blue skies
Eagle eyes scan Cheney Lake
Ripples on water

Eyes raised to heaven
Rest in the grace of blue skies
Sweet peace frees me

Blue skies beckon me
Take wings and fly higher
The eagle soars

Universal desire
Eagle soaring in blue sky
Wish to be eagle

Apples turning red
Summer coming to a close
Cider jars are clean

Dwayne Cole

Oh sweet redpoll wings,
red cap shining in bright light.
Look, love is spreading!

Is summer here indeed?
The green leaves quivering, yes.
Grebes float with clouds.

Coronavirus
Bringing us to our knees
A good place to pray

Rainbow archery
God's radiant clouds of care
Promises of security

The eye of God
The all-encompassing circle
Showing love for all

Double blessings
Security and hope
Shine on us

(Photo by Cole Thomas)

Walking in the rain
Rainbow arching over head
Who cannot be friends

Sometimes the whole sky
is a rainbow of color,
a fire dance of wonder.

Beauty to inspire!
Bedroom drapes are open wide.
Night-time clouds blush pink!

Moose below our deck
Cow parsnips big umbrellas
Light rain refreshing

Wing full of wonder—
Adventures are waiting.
Remember to breathe!

Grebes carry young under wings, up to 3 weeks,
until they are able to swim and find food on their own.

After three days of parental feeding, the young downy woodpecker has started pecking the peanuts on its own. They have ignored the sunflower heart seeds in the saucer. Before I put the peanuts out, the parents ate the seeds.

Nature's beauty clip
Tenderly feeding daughter
Parents are awesome

Slicing a ripe peach
Sweet juice trickling from knife blade
Nectar of the gods

Juice glistens on knife
A slice of sunrise in mouth
Nectar of the gods

When your world seems out of balance, upside down even,
go into nature and be still. See with new eyes.

Mother Nature's art
Right side up or upside down
Beauty to behold

Evening Romance

Low arc setting sun
Licks the snowy ice crystals
Mountain breasts blush pink

Goddess of the sun
Sol licks cotton candy cream
Artemus' breasts blush pink

Quiet please.
Leaves softly singing—
Art show in progress!

Spruce needles weaving
Ladder climbing into sky
A magical way

Sitting under spruce
gazing into blue skies
Awe inspired

A Divine moment
Not just for this hour in time
For all Eternity

Mother moose and calf
Tuned our spirit to tenderness
Oh gentle love

The light of beauty
Did not shine on us in vain
Deeper love for all
Sun, moon, stars, shine on all
Flowers blossom everywhere

In Autumn breeze
Birch leaves sing joyful tune
Geese are flying

Fall leaves are glowing
Moses had his burning bush
God's glory came down

Golden birch leaves
Heaven's glory is shining
Angels thinking light

Golden birch singing
Reaching for Robin egg skies
Inspire lofty thoughts

Lifts the human spirit
Ennobles the human soul
Nature's shrine for all

Silver birch trees
Minting golden coins
Climb and become

Humans must turn back
Hear shimmering leaves singing
Rediscover music

Welcome blue sky
Golden leaves singing
Let your light shine
My light is fading
Shine, shine on me

Dwayne Cole

As silent snow falls
Moose crunches tender twigs
Dinner music

The way the birch tree
threw snowballs down at the moose
Caused me to shiver

D. Cole

D. Cole

153

Ode to May

May, in Alaska, is one of my favorite months. All of nature
seems to be coming alive with beauty and wonder.
King salmon start returning to our streams announcing
the spawning season. Bears are coming out of winter hibernation
with little cubs rolling down the mountain sides
and tumbling over logs, all under mother's watchful eyes.
By mid-May, moose mothers will start giving birth to cute calves,
many twins, and a few triplets. Oh, the joy! Of spring in May.

> Some sing to entertain.
> I sing to keep bears away.
> I sing from treetops.

From my rocking chair
I witness a Steller's jay
Pounce on a nuthatch

A flash from blue sky
Red breast feathers dripping blood
A tear fell from eye

Theatre of beauty
Turning into jaws of hell
Church bells are silent

Wiping away tears,
I witnessed this scene—

Pine grosbeaks so dear
From Eden's garden singing
Heaven's bells ringing

Joyful gifts
    to lift
        and cheer

Sitting on my deck
Curling into your beauty
My soul is ripening

Each day is splendid
Shining with new light of day
Angels voices hoarse

Oh what a vision!
At heaven's door, sky is red.
Heaven's gifts descend

A knock at the door
Must lift the latch from within
Christ is risen!

Tidal flats appear
Window into our beginnings
Giver of life

Sea speaks without words
Gives answers to our questions
Explains universe

Sea, our dear Mother,
Giver of love more strong—
In us a song.

D. Cole

DwayneCole

Great One Rules

I walk across the tundra toward Denali
in a year of pandemic.
My soul crying out to heaven's angels.
Even the caribou grazing knows my sorrow.
The brown bear having blueberry desert
on the way to hibernation
feels the pain trickling down my cheeks.
There remains Denali, the Great One,
inviting me to play around her jeweled breast.
Open arms and breathe beauty and wonder.
Music of the spheres is playing love songs.
Nature warmly embraces grateful lovers.
Listen as Moses and Jesus listened to eternity.

Harmonious faith
Weeping endures for the night.
Joy comes in the morning

Denali and Tundra

Look across the tundra
Caribou and brown bear
Magnificence

God takes the paint brush
Wonder dances across tundra
Beauty is everywhere

Viewing these Denali scenes
Dreaming the first creation
How could I not say

Let my life become a landscape
gathering the light of heaven
Warming all in its glow

Denali sits beyond tundra
Ruling upon her throne
Great One everywhere

Inviting all to come
Play around jeweled breast
Gaze upon beauty

Like prophets of old
Climb to highest peak
Hear Divine speak

See world with new eyes
Where earth ends
Heaven begins

In mountains
One always receives
More than one seeks

Cherubim sing alleluia
Alleluia to Great One
Sees and feels everything

Bright sunny day
Tundra full of wildflowers
Great One glowing

The hiker's eyes moist
As she looks from Denali
Heaven is so near

Denali rises
Wrapped in snow blanket
Magical mystery

Returning to our condo
Where we have lived for 10 years—
See it for the first time

Photos taken summer of 2019 show tundra
with caribou, foothills with brown bear, and Denali—
formerly know as Mt. McKinley. Denali is
the highest mountain in North America
with a summit elevation of 20,310 feet
above sea level. Denali National Park has 6,075,107 acres.
Denali is 133 miles from Anchorage,
and normally has about 600,000 visitors each year.

The morning shines
White snow takes in the darkness
Purifying the world

Eyes raised to heaven
Rest in the grace of blue skies
Sweet peace frees me

Winter solstice
Darkest day in Alaska
Heaven's light shining

Sunrise illumines clouds
Tree limbs watching and waiting
Dreaming of new leaves

Nature is the poet.
Birds are poems nature writes—
Spreading songs of joy!

Bird eyes speak—
Wisdom from unknown realms.
Secrets of the heart!

Nature's characters
Extravagant beauty
Poetic joy

Dwayne Cole

Oh, mighty spruce tree
You inspire me to reach high
Clothed in blue sky

Each day I grow taller
Walking with the Sitka spruce
Filled with new dreams

Today I grow strong
Climbing with the giant spruce tree
Sprinkled with star dust

Geese calligraphy
Nature's golden handwriting
Setting sun magic

Wild geese honking
Above lenticular clouds
Crossing Cook Inlet

Who holds the compass
Charting annual migration
Captain of the seas

When the leader tires,
another takes his place.
Who calls for change?

Flying yesterday.
Wild geese honking day and night.
Who told them to fly?

Nature's Heart of Gold

Some say nature does not have a soul.
You live your life and I will live mine.

This piece of driftwood
sings—"Nature has a soul
and a heart of gold!"

Photo taken while walking on drive that leads to our
Alaska home. Witnessing this cloud, I sensed a deep feeling of
beauty. The wish to live and experience this beauty and wonder
is visible in all living entities. In sharing this beauty,
we experience enlivenment—The deep meaning of life. Nature
throbs with the desire to live. Haiku captures this beauty and
sense of adventurous enlightenment, luring us toward more
meaningful lives.

Heart Haiku is love
Hearts merging as one
Eternally

Look what we found
on the beach, Valentine Day.
Two hearts touching as one!

Heart Haiku
Holds and grows in tenderness
Heals hurt and brings peace

Rivers of Glaciers

Taking photographs
Rivers of glaciers flowing
Makes world real to us

Scenes hidden in past
Revealed in digital splendor
New life has been born

Rivers of glaciers
Not yet seen by humans
Nature's wonders!

Photos and poems
Ripen our love for all things
And for all people

Nature is driven by
Desire to have a future
To prolong itself

An unfolding cosmos
Each needing the feeling
of the other entity

All life has meaning
All entities have value
We are all one

Other Books By Dwayne Cole

Sharing kindness
in a world that needs healing—
Life's greatest purpose.

A Center that Holds: Adventures in Kindness
Alpenglow Miracles: Fire Dance of Wonder
A Prayer of Blessing: As You Go Remember This
A Relational Hermeneutic of Kindness
A Relational Trinity of Kindness
BEARS AND MOOSE OF ALASKA: Nature Poetry
Clouds of Inspiration
Down on the Farm in Georgia: A Poetic Memoir
Dragonfly Magic
Gentle Galilean Glories: The Tender Teachings of Jesus
God and Evil: An Ode to Kindness
Jesus' Transforming Beatitudes: Selected Sermons from Year A
Jesus' Transforming Love: Selected Sermons from Year B
Jesus' Transforming Gentle Teachings: Selected Sermons from Year C
Kindness Is Every Step
Lone Leaf Dancing
Poems Inspired by Process Philosophy
Poet of the Universe: A Vision of Beauty and
Goodness.
The Apostles' Creed: A Living Creed for the Living Church
The Bible: A Poetic Journey
The Book of Revelation: Jesus' Kindness Transforms Suffering
The Serenity Prayer: A Pathway to Peace and Happiness
The Story of the Bible: Authority, Inspiration, Canonization, and Translation
TREES AND DRIFTWOOD: Poetic Ecology
WINGS OF INSPIRATION

Images create
Reality waiting to be discovered
How we relate to world

Parson's Porch Books

Heart Haiku
ISBN: Softcover 978-1-955581-75-2
Copyright © 2022 by Dwayne Cole

Parson's Porch Books is an imprint of Parson's Porch *&* Company (PP*&*C) in Cleveland, Tennessee. PP*&*C is an innovative organization which raises money by publishing books of noted authors, representing all genres. Its face and voice is **David Russell Tullock** (dtullock@parsonsporch.com).

Parson's Porch *&* Company *turns books into bread & milk* by sharing its profits with the poor.

www.parsonsporch.com